SEX

AND THE

DECLINE

OF MONTANA

SEX

AND THE

DECLINE

OF MONTANA

* * *

daniel s. goodman

and

jim saucerman

ISBN 0-7414-3325-7

Published by:

INFI〇ITY
PUBLISHING.COM

1094 New DeHaven Street, Suite 100
West Conshohocken, PA 19428-2713
Info@buybooksontheweb.com
www.buybooksontheweb.com
Toll-free (877) BUY BOOK
Local Phone (610) 941-9999
Fax (610) 941-9959

Printed in the United States of America

Printed on Recycled Paper

Published June 2006

BOOKS BY:
DANIEL S. GOODMAN

I'LL TAKE SPIKED MUSTARD
I LIKE YOUR SHIRT
I'LL SPRING FOR LUNCH
I'LL HAVE MY USUAL

———————————

DEDICATED TO THE LATE
JIM SAUCERMAN,
CO-AUTHOR OF
SEX AND THE DECLINE OF MONTANA,
WHO PASSED AWAY BEFORE
THIS BOOK WAS PUBLISHED.

———————————

———————

THANKS TO GEORGE WEISS FOR HIS TECHNICAL
SUPPORT IN THE PRODUCTION OF THIS BOOK

———————

BILL OF FARE

GUYS NAMED STEWART

Take Al for example. Al's alright. Al might be your garage mechanic or just the guy next door, but Al's alright. Now Bob. Bob's good. You can say... "Hi Bob", or you can bob for apples, or you can bob your pet's tail. Bob's good. John? Yea, John works. You can say... "Hello, John" or you can go to the john. You would never call John, Jonathan, but John works. Chuck? Now there's a good one. First off you got ground chuck. Then there are woodchucks. You can chuck something at someone or tighten your drill bit into a chuck. And who doesn't like Chuck. Chuck is a good one. But Stewart? Stewart? Whose idea was that?

IT'S TIME TO CLEAN UP HIS ACT

A pal of mine just got fired from a dry cleaners for removing a spot from a garment. It was a 10 spot.

_____

MARITIME BRAINTEASER

What did the ocean say to the sun? Nothing. It just waved.

IS ANTIPASTO

a protest?

_____

I HAVE A QUESTION

If lemonade is for helpless lemons, what is foreign aid for?

MY FAVORITE EPITAPH ON A TOMBSTONE

Hey you with the mower...

———————

SPOOKY THOUGHTS

I wonder if the Karloffs ever named one of their daughters, Doris.

———————

ISN'T THERE A SONG CALLED, "NIGHT AND DAY"

Can you be knighted if you are in a daze?

SLIPPERS, SLIDERS, FLIPPERS AND FLAPPERS

Slippers are soft furry shoes in the shape of animals that you wear around the house. Why aren't slippers people who constantly mispronounce words or can't repeat a joke correctly? Sliders are what Navy guys call hamburgers onboard ship. Why aren't sliders sports figures who insist on diving across home plate to avoid being hit in the back of the head by a baseball? Flippers are webbed appendages on marine animals used for swimming through the water. Why aren't flippers people who make disgusting hand gestures at others when they feel offended? Flappers were young women in the 1920s that dressed up in ridiculous hats and dresses danced and caroused in the speakeasies. Why aren't flappers birds that take to the air rather than walk around our plazas and public places eating popcorn? This language makes no sense.

I WONDER WHAT TOM MC CANN WOULD SAY

During the Haight-Ashbury 1960's in San Francisco, a buddy said to a hippie in that district, "You have one shoe off. Did you lose one"? The hippie replied, "No, I found one. Can you help me find another one"?

IT WAS BORN IN AMERICA

and it came of age in America.

In an era when foreign competition threatens so many industries, it still sweetens our balance of trade.

The candy bar

JUST SAY NO TO DRUGS

I was wandering around the kitchen appliance section of Macy's last weekend and came across a rack filled with multi-colored squares referred to as silicon pot holders. Now first I'm thinking who in their right mind would smoke silicon pot? Second I'm thinking what are they doing selling this kind of thing at Macy's anyway?

REVENGE

Wouldn't it be strange to be a target reincarnated as a laser guided bomb?

THE PATIENT

Patient: I think I have literary talent.

Psychiatrist: Have your tried Tegrin?

———

RUBBER FOOD

I envision a joke shop someplace where you can buy a plate --- I don't mean a platter exactly but a serious plate that can be seen from across the room --- mounded with rubber food. It might be individual pieces of food or it could be one huge molded stack of food that clearly couldn't be consumed by anything less that a 500-pound Sumo wrestler who didn't eat for three months. I'm thinking mashed potatoes, Spanish rice, polenta, pasta shells and risotto overlain by half-a-slab of BBQ ribs, a turkey leg, some chicken pieces, a small filet, a few pieces of fruit, a little three-bean salad, one or two carefully arranged chunks of corn-on-the-cob, and assorted vegetables. Maybe the thing is even topped with rubber whipped cream and a cherry. Wouldn't that be funny?

LANDSCAPED CITY WHARF
(In Haiku)

Faded wooden planks
Vintage street lamps in a row
Rusted metal rails

Tour buses lined up
Cement walkways filled with trash
Pigeons on the hunt

Crowded restaurants
T-shirt bags filled with T-Shirts
Sun shades by the droves

MIDWEST MUSING

Why is Ohio high in the middle and not low in the middle?

———————

WATER SPORTS

Why do historians go on and on about Marco Polo when it's just a game in a swimming pool?

———————

IS IT JUST LEGEND OR TRUTH?

When General Douglas Mc Arthur waded ashore in the Philippines, did the chief honcho for the islands say, "Sorry, Doug, no receipt-no return".

MY ONE SLIVER OF SANITY

Laughter

———————

TRAFFIC

If they drilled a gigantic hole through a mountain and built a road for high-occupancy vehicles, would that lead to car pool tunnel syndrome?

BOOK TITLES YOU WON'T SEE

Chess For Dummies

———————

LAPSES OF MEMORY

You know how it is that from time to time you're talking to someone, and just can't remember the name of a person or object you need to refer to in your story? So rather than lose the thought you just plow right on through and say something like..., "How is old what's his name, anyway"? or "Would you please hand me that thing" or "Dear, are we out of wachamacallits?" Right.

Well, we've got two things in our master bedroom (yea, yea there's more than that – I'm just talking about these two that merit comment in this regard. First is that we have two tall storage units on each side of the bed for holding clothes. Each one of these units has a little pull out shelf that can be used to hold clothes while you store'em, or can be used as a night stand. The second thing is that we have two cats that pretty much have the run of the bedroom. They walk all over the head board, they stand or lay on these little shelves, and they sleep on the bed when we're not home.

So the other morning I'm getting dressed in the bedroom when my wife has one of these fleeting lapses of memory. She sticks her head around the corner and says... "Hon, would you please pull your thing out so the cats can walk on it?" This is not something I did that day.

EYE OF THE BEHOLDER

I am a person. That object over there is just a thing. I wonder if that thing thinks I'm just a thing.

CONDIMENTS

Can you spread embellishment on your hamburger?

———————

ON PUGILISM

If you are the undisputed heavy weight champion, what is everyone fighting about?

ON EDUCATION

History records that there was a time in the days of settlement of the great frontier when the focus of education was on readin' ritin' and 'rithmetic. As the country grew and towns and cities sprang up across the nation, life and education inevitably changed, becoming more complex and diversified. Eventually, topics such as art, history, medicine, astronomy, and interior decorating were adopted as vital components of the educational experience, expanding the scope of our learning far beyond the 3 Rs. At this point, however, I've begun to question whether this trend is really getting us anywhere.

To wit, I got a CAR-SORT mailer from my local extension course university last week that had no fewer than 185 pages of course offerings, including such things, as Advanced Dominoes, Extreme Sleeping, and Bowling as a Retirement Opportunity. While thumbing through the publication, I came across a course entitled, "Reproductive Methods". Now I mean, really. Reproductive Methods? As if the method we have coded into our genes is somehow flawed or inadequate, we have to actually study a bunch of things to figure out how to reproduce?

My vision is that the course would probably start with some historical perspectives, like in the early 1700s the French convention was for the male to bound from a platform elevated 60 feet above ground level, grab on a trapeze, and swing downward into the female at 113 miles per hour. The secondary objective here being to reach terminal velocity before the big event. By the 1960s, the image is probably that of the damsel reclining in a field of lime Jell-O wearing nothing but a pair of red high-cut tennis shoes, while Moonbeam strums his guitar and stares at the sun. Certainly, by the rocket age, the picture has to be that of the lady strapped to a 4 foot by 8 foot piece of ½-inch plywood secured at the end of a 2-mile long steel track on which rests a rocket sled ridden by Superman who departs Phoenix in the din, acccelerates to twice the speed of sound, and upon nearing this objective, unleashes his seatbelt as the sled slams to a halt covering the happy couple with bilge water. These are not things I need to know. It is unclear to me that we are moving in the right direction.

I TOLD A FRIEND

that he was a wonderful warm human being. He
replied, "How did you know my temperature?"

THE MAN IN WHITE

He was a tireless wanderer
He was a self taught genius of words
He was full of contradictions
He was a powerful life force
He was the people's author
He came and went on Haley's comet
He was Mark Twain

SOME ADVOCATE THAT

the traditional marriage vow, "for better or for worse" be changed to "for better or forget it".

———————

I HAVE A TWO HANDICAP

Me and my clubs

———————

DYSFUNCTIONAL

A friend of mine has a mother who is a bit of a messy housekeeper. Once when he was a youngster he tried to pee in the kitchen sink, but it was full of dirty dishes.

I WAS JUST WONDERING

Do you need glue to stick to a routine?

————————

DOES LUMBAGO

come with cream cheese?

A STEP INTO LIQUID

Surfing

_____

WHAT DID PRESIDENT HARRY S. TRUMAN SAY TO DOUGLAS MC ARTHUR?

"Doug, take a seat".

35 TO 1

Do you think it is contradictory when a horse player at a race track shouts, "That was a dark horse", after a long shot wins a race yet the color of the horse was light gray?

I'M NOT TALKIN ABOUT CARNATION MILK

My mother believed in reincarnation. She said, "Son, you'll come back as the front end of the horse".

MY DOCTOR TOLD ME TO CUT MY DRINKING IN HALF

So I cut out the water

———————

IS LASCIVIOUS

an advanced stage of lubricious or the other way
around?

JUST CURIOUS

Is a pedophilia a petite pedicurist?

I LOVE THIS 2 FOR 1 RESTAURANT SPECIAL

You pay for 2 meals but you get 1.

I'D LIKE TO OWN A B&B

Bar and Bordello

I THINK A WONDERFUL LOVER IS
SHOW BUSINESS

Once you feel the embrace, you may never get over it.

**SINCE NOAH WAS NOT A LICENSED
VETERINARIAN,**

I wonder if his job title was:

NATURAL ORGANIC ANIMAL HELPER

BORING

Restaurant or theatre critics who look upon themselves as EL CID

MY FAVORITE SHORT STORY

And in conclusion

———————

*** For Notes ***

*** For More Notes ***

*** For Closing Notes ***

*** Not For Notes ***